Tanka Left Behind
1968

*Tanka from the Notebooks of
Sanford Goldstein*

Keibooks, Perryville, Maryland, USA

Tanka Left Behind 1968, Tanka from the Notebooks of Sanford Goldstein

Copyright 2015 by Sanford Goldstein

Cover credit: "Two Watches." Copyright 2015 Kazuaki Wakui. Photo editor, Owen Smith, designer at Creative Kick. Used with permission.

ISBN-13: 978-1514848111
ISBN-10: 1514848112

Keibooks
P O Box 516
Perryville, MD 21903
http://AtlasPoetica.org
Keibooks@gmail.com

Table of Contents

Introduction

In my last two books, *Tanka Left Behind*, published in 2014, and published the same year *This Short Life : Minimalist Tanka*, I said in each introduction that it would probably be my last book. Now, here I am again with *Tanka Left Behind 1968*. I feel fairly certain this will be my last book as I turned 90 years of age in December 2014. Of course fate is perverse, and we shall see what we will see.

I am grateful as always to M. Kei for publishing some of my books. What I am finishing now is *Tanka Left Behind 1968*. I suddenly discovered this old notebook thrown under a pile manuscripts and quite stained with dust. I never intended to publish it when my wife was still alive. To have published a book about her illness would have embarrassed her, so even after she died in 1972, I hesitated. Forty-three years later and even before my own death, I decided to try to publish it.

What surprises me most is that I think *Tanka Left Behind 1968* is what I would call a tanka novel. The next to last tanka is a jolt, but I hope that readers do not rush to see it. It will be there waiting for them to finish this long tanka novel. I myself never look to see what the end of a novel I am reading is. To do so spoils what I call the anticipation of the end.

I have of course as in all my tanka revised the first drafts. Nothing has been added except that when I came to the end I added something that has jolted me all these many years and still does. Of course all the poems have been sharpened. I spill and then sharpen, sharpen and spill.

My collection concerns the most horrible summer of my life. We decided as a family to travel by car to Maine. We would head first to New York and see my wife's brother who was suffering from multiple sclerosis, a disease that results in a steady decline. First the fingers, then the eyes, then the inability to walk and the rest of one's life in bed. It was the first jolt. But staying at her brother's house not even a day, my wife had a sudden seizure and was then operated on. While she recuperated in the hospital on the second floor, my daughter Rachel fell from her bike and with a concussion was put on the third floor. As if each of these two events were not enough, I received a phone call that my father had died. We had sent our three children to Cleveland, for my wife's hospitalization was extensive.

So much for now, but I hope readers will read these poems in their proper order. As for me I bid my readers a fond farewell, unless I reappear in a tanka or two during the coming months.

Bon voyage, mes amis.
Sanford Goldstein

1968

whatever the doctors say
I know
the pain
of this long road
to recovery

these tears
I shed
for my wife,
I shed
for myself too

one by one
I eat my sparse
meals,
never miss
thinking about my wife

the tears
come
from my eyes,
not hers,
sick on her hospital bed

Tanka Left Behind 1968

the long silence
over the phone
talking
about the illness
of those we love

each fragment
of this long long
hospital day,
split even further
into fragments

no god
to pray to
I know,
still I pray for
her recovery

so much anguish
in her gentle
face
trying to frame
words

Sanford Goldstein

how long
before I forget
these long hospital days,
my wife
incoherent in bed

in the hospital
these long hours,
seems I live
by meal times
during painful days

one minute
the doctor speaks
of lumbar puncture,
the next
of baseball

each morning
along the hospital
corridor,
I pass a sweet old bag of bones
in a wheelchair

Tanka Left Behind 1968

all at once
she hums a tune
to herself,
my wife
on her hospital bed

incoherent
on her hospital
bed,
my wife unable
to speak with her eyes

in the tightness
of her hand
gripping mine,
I feel the life force
of loss

something
ethereal in her face
looking up
from her hospital
bed

today
one test
tomorrow another,
my wife's recovery seems to stretch
and snap back

the Negro
in the next bed
I watch,
her black hands
held up in prayer

stop
your eternal
analyzing
and let me hold
my wife's hand

what depth
of anxiety
behind her wrinkled
forehead,
my wife groping for words

Tanka Left Behind 1968

that line
of pain
circles her head
in the hospital
these days

my wife
on her hospital bed
asks for help,
we pronounce names
unable to remember who they are

today
helped my wife count
numbers,
one hundred and twenty
to three hundred

my only god
these days
the doctor,
he too keeps me
waiting

ten or more
times each day
I help my wife
through corridors
and back

silent
that old-timer in
his wheelchair,
he too sits and waits
for relief

at cafeteria
tables these days
I eat alone,
my thoughts on my wife
not on the food before me

tonight
at least
a few signs,
hoped-for coherence
from my wife

Tanka Left Behind 1968

I can only stumble
with my wife on the long road
to recovery,
July hot,
July hectic

I stand by her bed
but at a distance,
afraid, afraid,
to disturb some
hidden balance

tonight I cry
realizing again
this long road
of loneliness
that never ends

Venus
has her diabolical
uses,
her arteriovenous
malformation

for thirty years
it lay dormant in
her brain,
what caused
that sudden explosion?

nothing to do
but stand at a distance
and hope,
may my wife be able
to sleep

my son
as if from another world
comes to me,
a pain
in his ear

even in surgery
one must always walk
politically,
fingering the right
technique

Tanka Left Behind 1968

tonight
I'm smothered
in loneliness,
cannot see where
I am going

the laughter
by me, near me,
of other patients,
everything's trivial
except her hospital bed

I keep
these poems
and hope
she will read them
after recovering

nothing sweet
about the sympathy
from all sides,
I'm alone,
my wife on a hospital bed

existential choice,
I know
something
about it now considering
my wife's operation

in her eyes
that ask for something
of my consent,
I see once again
her love for me

not to be a monk
do I allow the doctor
with his knife,
her scalp shaved
for her life now

throbbing,
my head imagining
the doctor,
a knife on her
precious skull

Tanka Left Behind 1968

unable to see,
my wife uses
a roll
for butter,
her fingers faltering

by her bedside
on this hot July
night,
all my thoughts
on her lying there

I have
experienced
deep pits
of loneliness
in this hospital jungle

I question
those experts
again and again,
though I know
they will have to cut

trapped
and no longer trusting
even experts,
their scalpels
always on the alert

my tears fall
on the long ride
to the hospital
where my wife
lies without knowledge

I turn
to my wife's sister
with my own tears,
again those scalpels
trap me

I left her
smiling,
knowing only vaguely
something serious
will happen

Tanka Left Behind 1968

the eyes
she turns on me
seeking approval,
how that look
burns into my sockets

I see
the long pain
of innocence,
my wife looking out
over the white sheets

I recall
my wife waving
to me,
the stretcher rolls
down the long corridor

head shaved,
she tries through
broken words,
words I imagine
seeking approval

surgery over,
my wife's head
an inverted white bowl,
her eyes closed
in painless sleep

so cheerful
she was when
going to surgery,
asleep after the ordeal
and the waking in doubt

surgeon
so confident
in telling me,
yes he found
what caused the problem

each time
my hand touches
her head,
I will remember
the pain it underwent

Tanka Left Behind 1968

so cheerful
she was that morning
of surgery,
she knew, I believe,
where she was headed

years hence
I will remember
these horrific days,
visions of my wife
on her hospital bed

always
the question of whether
it was right to cut,
unable to escape
the dilemma I chose

tears less today,
and still still how tense
those five hours,
the surgery seemed
eternal and its continuation too

during
and after the horrible
surgery,
and still fewer tears
this long long day

and now
after surgery,
what changes
will I find in
her tender touch?

every hour
a long hurdle
these days,
my wife in
intensive care

her hand felt cold,
yes, eyes trying
to see,
behind her bandages,
what's going on?

Tanka Left Behind 1968

had we waited
that clot in her brain
might have burst,
and what continuous
damage then?

not once
did I pray to God
or Buddha,
even good news
can tangle into riot

the remainder
of my life
I fear,
and still
I have my wife

again in tears
I say I trust no man,
experts or not,
and still I obeyed
when they said cut

never
may she know
the constant pain,
the pain she underwent
on that hospital bed

these ten days
I have lived in my wife's
pain,
not from me will she know
the horrors of that time

after the bedtime story
and the singing of taps,
I tell my kids
to say a prayer
for their mother

my wife's face
swollen almost beyond
recognition,
she sleeps against
the railing of her bed

Tanka Left Behind 1968

sometimes
I sleep and dream
of my wife,
alone on her
hospital bed

these impersonal bills
demand exorbitant
sums,
what have they to do
with my ill wife?

never
will I be able to
erase
that sleeping face in pain
on a hospital bed

what tangled road
has she been on after
they cut her gains?
I explore signs that will
give me unknown answers

Sanford Goldstein

in-laws
finding their daughter
on that hospital bed,
oh this world of self
and self and self

I call her back
from some world
in her operation,
I look and look
for signals, for signs of awareness

on the bloated face
and in those blackened
eyes,
I see the face of my wife
before they cut her

only a few words
on that road back
from sedation,
yet tonight those words
bring a feeling of relief

Tanka Left Behind 1968

was that slight
movement of her head
a sign of recognition?
or did I imagine it
to speed my wife's recovery?

again and again
I call her name
and hope
she will come out
of that world of surgery

no one
deserves such pain
even in sleep,
my wife still bandaged
from surgery

slight
signs of recognition
today, tomorrow,
I do not cease
my hoping for more

my world
all blurred
and yet, yet,
I know my wife's
on that hospital bed

one arm swollen,
her face still bloated,
her head bandaged
eyes blackened and still
her gentle fingers on her right hand

my kids
splashing in their
uncle's pool,
why tell them of their
mother sleeping still

my kids
cling to me
these days,
I become their mother
for my sick wife

Tanka Left Behind 1968

they have
not seen their mother's
face,
too young to
ask questions

gentle to my kids,
not gentle to myself,
images remain
only of my wife's wrapped
head after the operation

so delicate
the brain remains
and yet it fights back
in the sparse words
of my wife

four times today
I tried to get words
from my wife,
she only stares at me
on her hospital bed

I walk
these lonely streets
waiting,
waiting for my wife's
recovery

all these men
with sideburns
down down,
is the look they garner
satisfaction enough?

again
sitting in the hospital
corridor,
waiting for the hour to pass
to have five minutes with my wife

that liquid
from that upside-down
bottle,
will it bring speech
to my silent wife?

Tanka Left Behind 1968

every summer
I'm trapped
by desire,
this summer my wife
on a hospital bed

I call and call . . .
into that deep world
of sleep,
my wife opens her eyes,
no words from her dry mouth

I am no saint
able to bring speech
to my wife,
eternal seems the silence,
eternal seems the pain

I fill out forms
for the endless
bills,
no end to them,
no end to my wife's silence

astronomical
these figures from
the forces of relief,
my wife only a bundle
of papers I sign for

even without words
my ill wife remains with
me,
I rub her cold
fingertips

today
signs of recognition,
how many miles to go
inside that deep
hospital world?

I wait
for my ill wife
to press my fingers,
to utter words
no longer soundless

Tanka Left Behind 1968

tonight
I know life's
a recovery,
it's from death I wait
for her knowing signs

a nurse
gives my wife tea
with a spoon,
how beautiful that
simple act of swallowing

I see a woman
unable to breathe,
her head cut too
I sigh over my wife's
continuing luck

in these
hospital corridors
I see a special world
I thought would
never pass me by

Sanford Goldstein

every phrase
from those dry lips
gives me hope
the damage of that cut
will not last forever

again and then again
I take my wife's weak hand
and look and look,
there must be a magic
something on her bloated face

a world
of re-learning
remains,
the damage from that
blood clot in her brain

when she awakes
let it be to see my face
and press my hand,
I blame myself enough
and want only something gentle

Tanka Left Behind 1968

up and down
on the hospital
elevator,
each moment I hope
brings my wife closer to relief

the eyes of that ill woman
next to the bed of my wife
has eyes to see with,
what dreadful visions
has she awakened from?

beautiful
the rain
tonight
outside this hospital
window

my wife,
does she see
the rain,
her wrist bound
to her hospital bed

the Negro
in this hospital room
prays to God,
I only look for signs
on my wife's face

the believer's prayer
of understood words
now over,
and still no signs
or prayers from my silent wife

the Negro
nods those understanding
words,
words not forthcoming
from my sick and silent wife

the only Christ
I have seen of late
is in those bound wrists,
both bound to
her hospital bed

Tanka Left Behind 1968

sad or not
tears
slide
from the corners of those eyes
of my wife on her hospital bed

drop by drop
from that suspended bottle
of liquid for health,
each drop finds its way
into my wife's arm

when she knows
they cut her scalp,
my hope remains,
will she finally take
my outstretched hand?

I want to believe
in that narrow hospital bed
something positive,
my wife, is she looking
at the falling rain?

the green
outside this hospital
window
looks much greener
in the falling rain

the record
of my wife's pain
can never reach
the pain
in my wife's bound wrist

tomorrow
will, I hope, be better
and still, still
that pain she must feel
in her bound wrist

in this forty-third year
they're out to get this fragile me,
my wife's brain
in battered surgery,
my kid with a concussion

Tanka Left Behind 1968

I feel
a fraction of what
that family felt,
crying in relief
the father was saved

at first shock
and then dramatics
and next self-pity,
but no mistaking those signs
in my daughter's eyes

I tell visitors
about my ill wife still asleep
and my hospitalized kid,
words, only words I know
for others have problems too

I continue
to see the road
of return
loaded with
dangerous snares

I want
to blame carelessness
yet cannot
seeing my child's fall
from a bike will be cured

once I read
when sorrows come they come not
as single spies,
ready and steady
to betray us all

no promise
in this my forty-third
year;
all the signs
point to down

beginning
to feel I won't reach
forty-four,
and now I curse
that selfish thought

Tanka Left Behind 1968

let them
remain safe now and later,
my wife and kid,
we will remain a family
of five now and forever

each drop
of milk my kid drinks
from this cup
suddenly means somehow
hope for my wife

pain
even from a twisted
word
comes out
in the eyes

today I help
my wife in her hospital bed
recover,
tomorrow, time
with my hospitalized kid

no collapse
in either my wife on two,
my kid on three,
and still still I fear
the rays of doom

nowadays
I neither argue
nor blame,
I wait for the next blow
in fear and trembling

tied to her bed
the sudden cry from
my wife,
startled, I know
by her hospital bed

my kid on her
third-floor hospital
bed
tries to remember
how she fell from a bike

Tanka Left Behind 1968

pulling
her white bandage
from her head,
my wife tries to
scratch and scratch

you gods
of instant doom
rub it in
with my wife and kid
on their hospital beds

no luck
for doom comes
by threes,
my wife and kid,
who I ponder is next?

like a kid
my wife tries to reach
the itch,
the incision
on her bald head

once I sang
"let my people go"
now I sing
for my wife
for my kid

each day
I lie and think on my large bed
in the brother's house,
things, things will be better
things have to be better

I feed
her soup like
a baby,
my wife open-eyed
on her hospital bed

like a prisoner
I wait, wait, wait
for my wife,
long and slow
hospital recovery

Tanka Left Behind 1968

each day
back and forth along
hospital corridors,
my wife on two,
my kid on three

fed my kid
on her hospital bed,
next my wife on hers,
sometimes outside
I munch a sandwich

no summer
riot is as long as
my mind's,
I wait and wait for
my child and wife to heal

I drink
deep during this eternal
summer
of endless surgery
endless pain

like drops
from an intravenous
bottle,
yet slower, still I wait,
wait and wait in the hospital

even
after surgery
and pain,
my cramped mind
whirls with desire

I realize
during this summer of
surgery and hospitals
that all of life is lonely
that all of life is sad

on a hospital bed
a quiet, sad Negro woman,
a gym teacher
no longer able to run
or use her hands

Tanka Left Behind 1968

at first
I thought of life,
only at first,
now I want more,
my wife not on a hospital bed

even
the ache between
my legs,
stilled, silent
these hospital days

though
the signs all point
to recovery,
still I see everywhere
no end, no erasures

so lonely
these days took
my three kids out
for a soda, my daughter
freed from her hospital bed

sutures out,
head bandaged
again,
I look longingly
at my hospital wife

the way
she greeted her old parents
like a child again,
my wife reborn on
her hospital bed

behind
those thick glasses
my wife's old father
holds back
a flood

my wife's mother
keeps repeating to us
poor Gloria
strange, Gloria
is my wife's sister

Tanka Left Behind 1968

even this bleak
summer of surgery
not as bleak
as that Negro lady's
lonely lonely smile

I risked all
when I let the doctors
use that knife,
at times my wife's coherent,
at times not at all

I see
the horseshoe
stitch
on my wife's
shaved head

although
her head's shaved,
the scar strange,
still I find that
my wife remains beautiful

this a summer
I cannot see my way
out,
and still let her rest
on that hospital bed

my big-eyed kid
on her hospital bed
hugs me,
never had I been hugged
like that before

my kid
breathes deep,
afraid,
she does not want to vomit,
leaving her hospital bed's her wish

to her mother
my wife keeps
repeating,
it's hard to see
it's hard to see

Tanka Left Behind 1968

in this dark
hospital room
no one sees
the spilled tears
on my grim hospital face

at last
I take my kid to her
temporary home,
for my wife it will take
much much longer

my wife
on her hospital bed
says *long long,*
she says it makes
the road much shorter

you powers
that break us all,
let me be,
keep me from selfishness,
keep me tuned to life

only
this hospital is not
a ghetto,
I see the beauty
of Negro faces

came to find
my wife's face thickly
powdered,
oh, this hospital madness
one day after another

she cried
for the first time
today,
are they tears
of my wife's recovery?

like Cinderella
I sit in lonely corners
waiting,
no magic in this
hospital room

Tanka Left Behind 1968

recalled
her address
today,
that's how far
my wife has come

I hold
my wife gently,
frightened,
she tells me
how glad she is I am here

always
words start on
my wife's lips,
I grope for signs
in this hospital room

the Negro lady
put talc on my wife's
back,
I see that as black
splendid power

my wife
cannot read the card
that says get well,
seeing the name of my aunt
I hide my tears from her

the way
my wife keeps
repeating,
David, Rachel, Lisa
David, Rachel, Lisa

I see
along these hospital corridors
signs of sympathy,
only disaster breaks
the barriers around us

even yesterday
when I saw those tears
in my wife's eyes,
and still life returning
is a long long road

Tanka Left Behind 1968

again and again
these steep hospital
stairs,
when too depressed
I take the elevator

on her arms
I see the many spots
left by needles
and I rub those arms
with white powder

eats
her custard
like a kid,
how gentle
the lifting of her spoon

we repeat
short sentences,
recall names,
our kids' ages
forgotten and learned

short,
very long,
right,
her garbled words
from her hospital bed

awake,
the pain worse
in her head,
relief
in a deep sleep

like a child
she stops talking
when strangers come
into her hospital
room

tonight
I laugh at
her garbled words,
I look down as she
smiles on her hospital bed

Tanka Left Behind 1968

even with
her head bandaged,
I feel intimacy
this long summer
night

lonelier
than ever
tonight,
even with the news
that my wife will recover

she garbled
the days again
garbled the months,
I see the worry
inside her bandaged head

kissing me
and saying she's
glad,
I let my wife
do as she wishes

thick
with desire
I pass lonely streets
on my way back
to my temporary house

endless
the way back
though shorter
than three terrible days
ago in my own pain

will
I ever let my wife
see
this journal
of pain?

munching
a sandwich and
having coffee,
thoughts only on
my sick wife

Tanka Left Behind 1968

drifting
asleep on her
hospital bed,
she repeats the days of the week
the months of the year

no lambchop
as beautiful as the one
she devoured
on her hospital
bed

touching
my face, ears,
neck, hair,
my wife smiling
on her hospital bed

even
in pain there
is beauty,
my wife her head
still bandaged

Sanford Goldstein

so concentrated
in the way she eats
her meal,
part of the long road
back from surgery

and still
the hours pass
while I wait,
I wait on a chair
in this hospital room

through
the gauze I see
hair sprouting
from my wife's
damaged head

her head
bandaged and speech
not yet restored,
my wife in bed
tries her harmonica

Tanka Left Behind 1968

more precious now
than at any other point,
precious wife,
your damaged brain
is on the way to being mended

closer than ever
to that disaster in your brain,
I still hope,
I still go about in a daze
aware always of your presence

not once
did I call
on unearthly aid
during these hospital days,
my faith only in her surgeon

she presses
down hard even now
on her bandage,
I feel she must be trying
to stop the incessant pain

my wife
shows signs of
recovery,
on that nearby bed
I see a despondent Negro

for three hours
my kids waiting in
corridors,
all that time
I visited my wife

each
goodnight sends me
away sad,
I step quietly, secretly,
I know tomorrow I will be back

each movement
I take during these hospital
days,
I have the feeling
someone is trying to get me

Tanka Left Behind 1968

waved
a sign of love
to my kids
again I am on my way
to the hospital

cried
last night after sending
my kids to Cleveland,
they will wait at their grandparents'
home until my wife and I return

again
her bandage
askew,
kid-like my wife
in her hospital room

how my wife
pleads for a cigarette
in her bed,
so like a kid pleading
for the candy she desires

we stumble
over words in
a newspaper,
unable to read my kids'
farewell note to her

we stumble
over words on
that long road,
the road beyond
surgery has to be faced

says
she wants to smoke
the bedpan,
such a fierce storm
in my wife's mind

never
saw the atomic bomb
until surgery,
survival but without
real contentment

Tanka Left Behind 1968

she stood
by her bed to show the robe
sent to her
by my parents
and my kids in Cleveland

sounds
of New York through
this Bronx window,
she gathers them in
without analysis, without pain

I sit
on this corridor
sofa,
writing poems
about my wife

I have never
prayed to any
God,
and still I know
someone saved my wife

my three kids
seem a lifetime
away,
so long ago on the plane
leaving my wife and me behind

so firm
the grip of her delicate
hand,
no operation can cut away
the love we have

her plea
for a Lucky Strike
on her sick bed,
another battering
of my weak heart

is her childlike
state a special phase
of her disease,
I will continue and continue
to try to make her well

Tanka Left Behind 1968

remembering
snatches of songs,
of poems,
when will my wife's brain
snap into memory

all
my waking hours
directed to her,
and still longings
of desire remain

seven cigarettes
today was her plea
and tomorrow ten,
but when will memory
increase as a get-well sign

tears for her brother,
her uncle and three kids,
a plea again and again,
but nothing about word loss
and the brain gone astray

all day
she says she's glad
and still, still,
tears keep spilling
on her hospital bed

what wanderings
rush through my wife's
confused brain,
she lies on her bed
this long summer night

said
her children remain near
though gone so far,
even this long long month
seems millions of miles off

my wife walks,
talks, sings, asks,
and still still
memory eludes her
and haunts me

Tanka Left Behind 1968

I have given up
miracles I no longer
expect,
eager I am more and more
my wife will regain her memory

her forgetting
makes each date
poignant,
am I forgetting
even my own wishes?

news of
soon going home
I tell my wife,
how her face brightens
on her hospital bed

the reason
for that horseshoe scar
on her head,
at last this afternoon
I try to explain it again

crying
after the phone call
to our kids,
she tells me how sad
to be separated from them

how eager
she is to regain
memory,
how sad she is
unable to remember a name

so many
kisses to my wife
today,
how much there is
for her to relearn

like a kid
she cries when I take
her matches away,
she knows she should
not smoke too much

Tanka Left Behind 1968

again I repeat
for her to remember
the cause,
arteriovenous
malformation

even three memories
are like a million to my ill
wife,
again and again she tries
to remember her brother's kids

soon a week
of rest outside
the hospital,
will being together
on our own bring her peace?

tears and more tears
trying to remember where
she works,
nor does she remember
what she teaches

yes sometimes
what she remembered
is soon forgotten,
again tears assail
my hospitalized wife

a thousand times
she tells me she's glad
I came,
her precious eyes
can never deceive me

how cruel
to repeat and repeat
the same names,
I try to force memories
from my hospitalized wife

no last rites
are these forced
confessions,
my wife knows
no world but now

Tanka Left Behind 1968

tonight
I tasted cruelty
and desperation
in the angry phone call
from her parents

for one month
I have always passed through
these New York streets,
and still I hold on to what
I know is sane for wretched me

let this night pass
and may my ill wife
sleep
no seizures may there be,
and I will kiss her when she wakes

every corner
this Saturday night
sick with desire,
I follow the signs
that will lead me home

let no record
of this terrible month
of pain be lost,
my poems will bear
witness to what we endured

such insanity
to dig up the past
again and again,
and still I do, but not to
hurl it at some sick vegetable

frantically
the words tried
to pour out,
blocked they were
from my poor wife's gaze

again and again
she kisses
these hands,
I hold her own
in gratitude

Tanka Left Behind 1968

left her calm
tonight and returning
found her calm,
even as I write my tanka
I let the quiet pass through

so joyful
talking over the phone
to her youngest
now four years old,
smiles around the hospital room

signs
of a return to the normal
for my wife,
how vivid that scar
on her scalp

that hair
shaved like a Buddhist
nun's
so peaceful
my wife's smile

Sanford Goldstein

one after
another she smokes,
my wife on a bench
we are about to leave
this dreary hospital world

listening
to talk of other
operations,
she sits quietly
even with her head shaved

how distant
our three kids gone
this quiet night,
long gone to Cleveland,
and my wife on her hospital bed

eager to please
she drinks her bedtime
juice,
like a kid she finishes,
afraid to be scolded

Tanka Left Behind 1968

such joy
in her recognition
of words,
she saw them in a newspaper ad
lying on her bed

tears tonight
over the long length
of her hospital life,
agonies recalled a while
and then a long silence

soon
our departure from
her hospital room,
two weeks of quiet
at a nearby motel

she is calm
waiting for release
from this room,
my mind on some quiet
motel room close to the hospital

a sudden call
as if the pain was
not enough,
my father dying
in his house in Cleveland

how gray
the night sky,
gray my thoughts
on this long night flight
to Cleveland

I had to lie
to my precious wife
I could not visit
telling her I had to help
her mother buy a girdle

no way out
these days with my wife
on her hospital bed,
my dad about to be
buried in distant Cleveland

Tanka Left Behind 1968

all
my love for my mother
spilled out
in the hospital corridor
over the phone

still not enough?
my daughter once hospitalized
a floor above her mother's,
and now now now my father
about to be buried in Cleveland

so many weeks
my world broken, tossed,
no end in sight,
and still the worries
continue to pile up

once I cried
when a president
was assassinated,
now I cry for my wife,
my daughter, and my dad

each moment
some new pain
grabs hold,
and still I do not break,
do not collapse

I wait
for the midnight
plane
to take me to
the funeral of my father

I drink coffee,
eat some apple pie,
write tanka,
and my father lying
in some funeral home

I left her smiling
in the hospital corridor
avoiding truths,
I head home by plane
for my father's funeral

Tanka Left Behind 1968

no shaving tonight,
I board the midnight plane
in old clothes,
my father dead,
my mother in grief

lately
everything makes me
cry,
children on the plane
and scolded by mothers

life
carries me where
it will,
swinging through silence
and pain these many days

everything
downhill these
days,
disasters,
crushing the now of my life

it takes
so much courage
these days,
life kills and kills
and endless hospital bills

from somewhere
I need fortitude and skill,
I need strength
to pass my father
in his casket, closed, I hope

that flat tire
in the taxi taking me
to my mother,
no accident that,
somebody wants me dead

the face
I turned toward
death
wants to close
its weary eyes

Tanka Left Behind 1968

in the home
the taxi takes me to,
my mother there,
in tears and fearful
at least my kids will be waiting

tonight
I feel lonely about many people,
for my dad too,
yesterday I was in New York,
today, in the early morning, I am in Cleveland

all that talk
as if my father in his casket
never was,
how sad these funeral
customs so close to home

the entire funeral
found me exhausted, inert,
I hold my mother's hand,
the casket is closed,
my father's face not seen

I remain steady
to give my mother
strength,
my insides feel as if
I am bursting

on a night stand
his Camel cigarettes
and pills in a bottle,
remains of a father I know is dead,
a father who never noticed me

back turned
from the house where
my kids sit in silence
my youngest has no idea
of death or prayer or loss

all five of us stuffed
into a black limousine,
told to sit, move,
my mother wants me
and I sit next to her

Tanka Left Behind 1968

at times
during the funeral
day,
I talk about my wife,
still on her hospital bed

a phony sermon
about my dead father's life
maybe the speaker knew,
what was left unsaid, unspoken,
could never be uttered

glad
the casket remained
closed,
the shadows of a life
of shame stream down

the casket lid
was never opened,
my father inside,
what was the face of
my father in death?

greetings
to strangers
table talk,
handshakes
and words somehow

my three kids
all silent in their seats,
their first death,
I watch their faces,
stern, serious, all of us

all the talk
as if my father never
was,
his reality was a mystery
except for those few of us who knew it

death
inches toward me,
my father gone,
how close my wife came to death
but saved somehow by courage

Tanka Left Behind 1968

in borrowed
old clothes to give
the right effect,
I endure in silence
the death of my father

I imagine
my mother all alone
in that big house,
I know how loneliness
does its sordid work

hugging
my three silent
kids,
the day has gone
and I must return to my wife

life is like that,
one minute a person's gone,
the next endurance,
and still, still, my precious wife
remains on her hospital bed

I return
and prepare my wife
to go to the motel,
I buy her a large hat
to hide her baldness

so strange
my wife's downward look
in her floppy hat,
the hat hides her scar
and we smile at each other

in two moments
all was changed for me and my kids
and my wife's battered brain,
surgery that had to be done soon,
my father gasping out his end

on the return
from my father's
funeral,
two drunks kissing
on a Negro corner

Tanka Left Behind 1968

for two weeks
at the cheap motel we stay at,
my wife takes her pills
I watch and hope for signs,
I bring supper to her at the motel

in this motel room
waiting for my wife to recover,
I think and hope,
how lonely my mother must be,
how confused my three kids

I wait
to tell my calm wife
about my father,
we talk about our kids,
how my wife wants them by her

afraid to disturb
some hidden balance,
we hold off,
close to her in bed,
my arm around her side

over the phone
my mother offers
encouragement,
my kids tell us they miss us
they miss me, miss their mother

I listen
to my wife trying
the Beethoven,
her head sways to the rhythm,
her hand tightly in mine

precious
each day being with
my wife,
her brain struggling
to bring words and memories

each day
short wisps
of hair,
they curl and curl
over her violent scar

Tanka Left Behind 1968

almost ten days
at the pleasant motel where we hope
to get freed by the hospital,
I finally tell my wife by my side
about the death of my father

when the crisis
that brought me to confront
death,
all my Zen
collapsed, fell apart

where
was no-thought, no dispersal
when the crisis came?
when those three events
came to halt me in my path?

I said
Beloved Buddha
each night,
and I listed the names I knew
of all who died during my life

I supply words
even on the fourteenth day
at the motel,
the hospital frees us
and we reserve seats on a plane

yes, we will move on
from New York to Indiana,
from confusion to hope,
our kids will remain
another week in Cleveland

these hot
autumn days at our house
I spend with my wife,
on the road back from pain,
from surgery, from separation

this morning
from the brown vase
on the kitchen table,
I remove the withered flowers
and buy fresh ones at a shop

Tanka Left Behind 1968

soon time for school
and time for the kids
too,
my wife and I prepare
our September university classes

how happy
our three kids to find
us together,
I hold off disciplining
the three of them

I know I can teach
but wonder about my wife
whose operation —
well, all words were split
and so she cannot read

faces
were split too
only one half seen,
I try looking out of one eye,
I know even that is difficult

the road ahead
lies scattered with
fears,
I firmly hold her hand,
she firmly holds mine

Afterword

Now ninety years old, Sanford Goldstein is the foremost tanka poet writing in English today. In *Tanka Left Behind 1968*, he gives us a glimpse into his early life and development as a poet. 1968 was a turbulent time when the poet's wife was hospitalized with a serious brain disorder, his daughter was hospitalized after a bicycle accident, and his father died.

Through it all, Goldstein was aware of the outside world with its protest marches and civil rights issues. The black nurses and patients at the hospital are part of the constrained intimacy of that time, each family consumed by their private griefs, yet sharing a common humanity. As may be expected for a journal written in 1968, Goldstein's language is sometimes dated, but that too is part of the era. Now, nearly fifty years later, looking back as he writes his introduction, he gives us perspective on his literature and his life.

M. Kei

Biographies

Born in 1925, Sanford Goldstein has written many books of tanka, including *This Tanka World*, his first book in 1977. His latest book before *Tanka Left Behind* was *This Short Life : Minimalist Tanka* (Keibooks, 2014). His other works include short stories, essays, co-translations of famous Japanese tanka writers, including *Tangled Hair* by Akiko Yosano (1971) and Takuboku Ishikawa's *Romaji Diary and Sad Toys* (1985) (these translations with Seishi Shinoda).

Kazuaki Wakui is an artist, essayist, photographer, and cartoonist of manga (Japanese-style humour).

M. Kei is a tall ship sailor and award-winning poet who lives on Maryland's Eastern shore. He was the editor-in-chief of *Take Five : Best Contemporary Tanka, Vols. 1–4*, the editor of *Bright Stars, An Organic Tanka Anthology, Vols. 1–7*, and the editor of *Atlas Poetica : A Journal of World Tanka*. His most recent collection of poetry is *January, A Tanka Diary*.

Praise for Tanka Left Behind 1968

"What an unexpected delight. I thought I knew well the oeuvre of Sanford Goldstein. But *Tanka Left Behind 1968*, while not a new theme, does bring to the long illness of his wife a new immediacy. This book, written as its events unfolded, was never meant for publishing, not during his wife's lifetime nor his own. But here in his 90th year, Goldstein has relented of this resolve and gives us in this 'tanka novel' one of his most moving and powerful works. A classic from the father of English tanka, written in his apparently artless style, just when we thought we'd heard all he had to say. This is absolutely essential Goldstein. A must have for any English tanka collection."

—Larry Kimmel, editor of Winfred Press

"Sanford Goldstein's latest collection, *Tanka Left Behind 1968*, contains some of his earliest tanka. Goldstein, in his introduction to this collection, refers to it as a "tanka novel" inasmuch as the poems are arranged in a narrative structure that allows such a reading. The first time I read the collection, I did so in a single session without leaving my chair. These extraordinarily plain spoken and terse poems are at the same time emotionally powerful, gripping one's attention and one's sympathy, and astonishingly beautiful in their soul-baring honesty. There is simply no other work of tanka in English with which to fairly compare this collection. I highly recommend this book to all poetry-lovers and doubly so to those with an interest in tanka verse. In its pages, you will witness the power of Sanford Goldstein's incomparable tanka, even in their earliest years."

—Denis M. Garrison, author of *First Winter Rain*, and publisher of the first edition of Sanford Goldstein's collection of collections, *Four Decades on My Tanka Road*

Made in the USA
Coppell, TX
10 October 2021

63815076R00059